910.91
BIS   Biskup, Agnieszka.

Exploring Titanic

32335104001880

DATE DUE	BORROWER'S NAME	ROOM NUMBER

910.91 $29.99
BIS
Biskup, Agnieszka.

Exploring Titanic : An Isabel Soto History Adventure

32335104001880
CHICAGO PUBLIC SCHOOLS
MCAULIFFE ELEMENTARY SCHOOL
1841 NORTH SPRINGFIELD AVE
CHICAGO, IL 60647
RL: 4.4
PTS: 0.5
Quiz: 131449

GRAPHIC LIBRARY™

GRAPHIC EXPEDITIONS

EXPLORING TITANIC

AN *Isabel Soto* HISTORY ADVENTURE

by Agnieszka Biskup

illustrated by Al Bigley and Bill Anderson

Consultant:
Karen Kamuda, Vice President
Titanic Historical Society and Titanic Museum
Indian Orchard, Massachusetts

Capstone
press®

Mankato, Minnesota

Graphic Library is published by Capstone Press,
151 Good Counsel Drive, P.O. Box 669, Mankato, Minnesota 56002.
www.capstonepub.com

Books published by Capstone Press are manufactured with paper
containing at least 10 percent post-consumer waste.

Library of Congress Cataloging-in-Publication Data
Biskup, Agnieszka.
    Exploring Titanic: an Isabel Soto history adventure / by Agnieszka Biskup ;
        illustrated by Al Bigley and Bill Anderson.
    p. cm. — (Graphic library. Graphic expeditions)
    Summary: "In graphic novel format, follows the adventures of Isabel Soto as she
investigates the sinking of the Titanic" — Provided by publisher.
    Includes bibliographical references and index.
    ISBN 978-1-4296-3410-6 (library binding)
    ISBN 978-1-4296-3892-0 (paperback)
    1. Titanic (Steamship) — Comic books, strips, etc. — Juvenile literature. 2. Shipwrecks
— North Atantic Ocean — Comic books, strips, etc. — Juvenile literature. 3. Graphic novels.
I. Bigley, Al, ill. II. Anderson, Bill, 1963– ill. III. Title. IV. Series.
G530.T6B587 2010
910.9163'4 — dc22   2009004954

Designer
Alison Thiele

Cover Artist
Tod G. Smith

Colorist
Michael Kelleher

Media Researcher
Wanda Winch

Editor
Aaron Sautter

Photo Credits: AP Images/Nauticus, 25; Getty Images Inc./Hulton Archive, 17;
    Shutterstock/Jurgen Ziewe, 19

Design Elements: Shutterstock/Chen Ping Hung (framed edge design); mmmm (world
    map design); Mushakesa (abstract lines design); Najin (old parchment design)

Printed in the United States of America in Stevens Point, Wisconsin.
082010
005920R

TABLE OF CONTENTS

The International History Museum, present day

Thanks for coming so quickly, Izzy. We need your help for our new exhibit. Come to my office, and I'll explain.

FLAP FLAP FLAP FLAP

Lead the way.

INTERNATIO HISTORY MUSEUM

The new exhibit is about the *Titanic*. I'm sure you know about it?

Of course! It's one of the most famous ships of all time. It sank on its very first voyage.

Titanic is the largest passenger steamship in the world. Fully loaded, she can carry 3,500 passengers and crew.

She is 175 feet, or 53 meters, tall. That's as high as a 17-story building.

The ship is 882 feet, or 269 meters, long. That's nearly the same length as four city blocks.

Titanic has four funnels. Each one is big enough to drive two trains through. The first three funnels are chimneys for the coal furnaces. The fourth funnel brings fresh air into the engine rooms.

She can cruise at a speed of about 21 knots. That equals about 24 miles, or 39 kilometers, per hour.

I notice there are only 20 lifeboats. That isn't enough room for all the people onboard, is it?

No, but don't worry. We actually have four more lifeboats than the law requires. Now let me show you how beautiful Titanic is on the inside.

No expense has been spared for the *Titanic*. She has all of the modern comforts, including electric lights and heating.

The grand staircase has a glass dome above it to let in natural light.

The first-class dining room seats more than 500 people and serves the finest foods. The second-class and third-class passengers have separate dining areas.

First-class passengers can also enjoy a modern gymnasium and a swimming pool. It's one of the first pools to be included on an ocean liner.

Hmm. The W.I.S.P. says that the British ship RMS *Carpathia* rescued the *Titanic* survivors on April 15, 1912.

I should talk to some of the survivors. They should know exactly what happened.

RESCUE AT SEA

Just after midnight on April 15, 1912, RMS *Carpathia* received a distress call from *Titanic*. The *Carpathia* was more than 50 miles (80 kilometers) away. Captain Arthur Rostron raced his ship through dangerous ice fields to get to the *Titanic*. But *Carpathia* couldn't reach *Titanic* before it sank. At about 4:00 the following morning, *Carpathia's* crew picked up 705 *Titanic* survivors. Rostron and his crew were considered heroes because of their quick response to the disaster.

But at 11:40 in the evening, lookout man Frederick Fleet spotted an iceberg right ahead of the ship. Orders were given to turn the ship, but it was too late. The ship's right side grazed the iceberg. A few minutes later, *Titanic* came to a dead stop.

SCREEEEEECH!

DEADLY ICE

Only about 10 percent of an iceberg is visible above water. Below the water's surface, an iceberg's sharp edges can puncture a ship's hull.

At first, people didn't think the situation was very serious. The first lifeboats weren't even half-full when they were lowered.

But things soon became chaotic. Distress flares were sent up to alert ships in the area. The ship's band played music to help keep people calm. Those brave men kept playing until the ship went down.

I got on one of the last lifeboats. No rescue ship was in sight. There was little hope left for anyone still on the *Titanic*.

CRAAACK!

Several studies were done on the ship's iron rivets.

How did the rivets contribute to the ship sinking?

Many of the rivet heads popped off when the ship hit the iceberg.

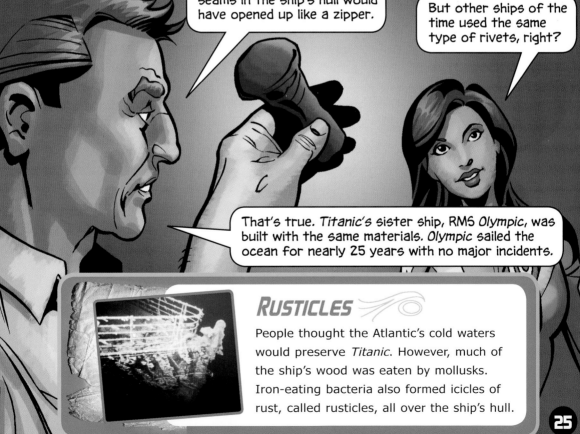

After the rivets broke, the seams in the ship's hull would have opened up like a zipper.

But other ships of the time used the same type of rivets, right?

That's true. *Titanic's* sister ship, RMS *Olympic*, was built with the same materials. *Olympic* sailed the ocean for nearly 25 years with no major incidents.

RUSTICLES

People thought the Atlantic's cold waters would preserve *Titanic*. However, much of the ship's wood was eaten by mollusks. Iron-eating bacteria also formed icicles of rust, called rusticles, all over the ship's hull.

The International History Museum, present day
I hope my report helps your exhibit, Tom.
Your research is fantastic, Izzy. It sounds like a terrible chain of events led to the tragedy.
The impact speed, cold temperatures, and outdated lifeboat laws all add up to a tragic story.
But some good did come from the disaster.

After the *Titanic* disaster, ships were required to have lifeboat space for every person onboard.

Safety drills were also required so the crew and passengers would know what to do in an emergency.

Ships began using radios around the clock.

In 1914, the International Ice Patrol was established. It tracks icebergs in the North Atlantic and alerts ships to any dangers.

Disasters can still occur at sea. But the safety measures put in place after the *Titanic* sank have helped save many lives.

In the early 1900s, two of the biggest shipping companies were the Cunard Line and the White Star Line. Cunard ships were the fastest. The White Star Line competed for passengers by building the biggest, most comfortable ships in the world. *Titanic* was to be the biggest of them all.

The RMS in RMS *Titanic* stands for Royal Mail Steamer. One of the ship's duties was to pick up and drop off mail each time she stopped at a port.

More than 1,500 people died when *Titanic* sank. The largest losses were among the third-class passengers and the crew. Third class, also known as steerage, was located in the lower levels of the ship. Many third-class passengers died because they couldn't reach the lifeboats on the upper decks in time.

Several famous millionaires were passengers on *Titanic*. These included John Jacob Astor, Benjamin Guggenheim, and Isidor Straus. Joseph Bruce Ismay, the managing director of the White Star Line, was onboard as well. Astor, Guggenheim, and Straus did not survive the disaster.

Titanic was one of the first ships to use the SOS signal, which is the international distress signal for ships in need of urgent help.

Waves that hit an iceberg help show its position, especially at night. When the sea is calm, icebergs are very difficult to spot in the dark.

The lifeboats on *Titanic* only had room for 1,178 people. Many of the first lifeboats were lowered only partially filled. If the lifeboats had been completely filled, almost 500 more people could have been saved.

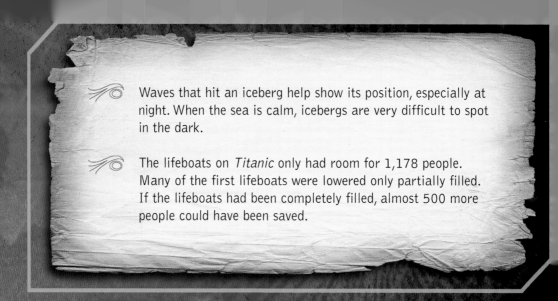

MORE ABOUT

Isabel Soto

NAME: Dr. Isabel "Izzy" Soto
DEGREES: History and Anthropology
BUILD: Athletic **HAIR:** Dark Brown
EYES: Brown **HEIGHT:** 5' 7"

W.I.S.P.: The Worldwide Inter-dimensional Space/Time Portal developed by Max Axiom at Axiom Laboratory.

BACKSTORY: Dr. Isabel "Izzy" Soto caught the history bug as a little girl. Every night, her grandfather told her about his adventures exploring ancient ruins in South America. He believed lost cultures teach people a great deal about history.

Izzy's love of cultures followed her to college. She studied history and anthropology. On a research trip to Thailand, she discovered an ancient stone with mysterious energy. Izzy took the stone to Super Scientist Max Axiom, who determined that the stone's energy cuts across space and time. Harnessing the power of the stone, he built a device called the W.I.S.P. It opens windows to any place and any time. Izzy now travels through time to see history unfold before her eyes. Although she must not change history, she can observe and investigate historical events.

bow (BAU) — the front end of a ship

compartment (kuhm-PART-muhnt) — a section inside a ship that is divided by watertight walls and doors

exhibit (eg-ZIB-it) — a display that shows something to the public

flare (FLAYR) — a burst of light shot from a gun to announce one's presence or position

funnel (FUHN-uhl) — a smokestack on a steamship

hull (HULL) — the main body of a ship

iceberg (EYESS-berg) — a huge piece of ice that floats in the ocean; icebergs break off from glaciers.

immigrant (IM-uh-gruhnt) — someone who comes from one country to live permanently in another country

oceanographer (oh-shuh-NOG-ruh-fer) — a scientist who studies the ocean and ocean life

rivet (RIV-it) — a strong metal bolt that is used to fasten something together

sonar (SOH-nar) — a device that uses sound waves to find underwater objects; sonar stands for sound navigation and ranging.

SOS (ESS OH ESS) — a signal sent out by a ship or a plane to call for urgent help

stern (STERN) — the back end of a ship

wireless (WIRE-lis) — a device that uses radio waves to send telegraph messages

READ MORE

Adams, Simon. *Titanic.* Eyewitness Books. New York: DK, 2009.

Ballard, Robert D. *Exploring the Titanic: How the Greatest Ship Ever Lost — Was Found.* Toronto, Ont.: Madison Press Books, 2009.

Crosbie, Duncan. *Titanic: The Ship of Dreams.* New York: Orchard Books, 2007.

Jenkins, Martin. *Titanic: Disaster at Sea.* Cambridge, Mass.: Candlewick Press, 2008.

Pipe, Jim. *Titanic.* Richmond Hill, Ont.: Firefly Books, 2007.

Temple, Bob. *The Titanic: An Interactive History Adventure.* You Choose Books. Mankato, Minn.: Capstone Press, 2008.

INTERNET SITES

FactHound offers a safe, fun way to find Internet sites related to this book. All sites on FactHound have been researched by our staff.

Here's all you do:

Visit *www.facthound.com*

FactHound will fetch the best sites for you!

INDEX